The Beauty of Life

The Beauty of Life

By Teri Hines

© Copyright 2024 Teri Hines

Contact Teri Hines or invite her
to speak at your next engagement:
Email - teri.hines03@gmail.com

Published by:

Maximized Productions, UPH Div.
6715 Suitland Road
Morningside, Maryland 20746
www.unlockpublishinghouse.com
ISBN:979-8-9875001-4-9

Unless otherwise indicated, Bible quotations are taken from:

New King James Version *(NKJV): Scripture taken from the New King James Version®. Copyright © 1964 by Thomas Nelson. Used by permission. All rights reserved.*

Printed in the United States of America 2024

Table of Contents

Dedication   9

Prayer   10

Purpose   11

Intent   12

Jewels of the Heart   13

Breath of Life   16

All Things Are Possible   20

What is Faith   22

Why am I Still in Chains   26

Why am I Felling This Way   31

Deep Sea Diving   34

The Big Spirit in the Sky   39

My Cry to the One who Hears   44

He Who Wore a Crown of Thorns   49

Up From the Ashes   52

The Sea of Life   57

Mister Man   61

Do You Know   65

Love is Not the Color of My Skin   68

Saved by Him   72

Sum of it All   75

The Treasure of Life   79

Love is our Manifesto   83

He Who Lives   85

Suicidal Hot Line   88

Prayers   89

Blessings   90

Protection   91

Peace   93

Guidance   95

Abide   96

The Word of God   97

Dedication

This book is dedicated to the memory of my beloved father and mother but inspired by the Holy Spirit for the glory of God through our Lord Jesus Christ.

Prayer

Heavenly Father,

We come before You, asking for repentance that our hearts may turn and recognize You as Holy and unblameable throughout all Your works. You are the Creator of all humanity and even the times we are now living in. Dreadful events are happening before our eyes, so we are calling out to You. We are in dire need of You and we need You now more than ever.

Man's duty is to call on You and bless Your Holy Name. You are God and God alone, and there is no help in another. Hopefully, we will bend our knees in prayer, petitioning for help in these times. Father God, You have instructed us to pray without ceasing[1]. You also said in Your Word to watch and pray, lest we enter into temptation[2]. Father touch our hearts that we may find ourselves in a posture to repent. We are in an alarming cry for Your help.

Father, we pray for peace and protection over us in the United States. Holy Spirit, would You lead and guide us through these trouble times.

Lord, we love and thank You.
In Jesus' Name.

[1] **I Thessalonians 5:17**
[2] **Matthew 26:41**

Purpose

The purpose of this book is to reflect on the goodness of God and realize that His lovingkindness is better than life.[1] When we become faithless and uncertain about our journey, we know that God our Father is walking with us. He said in His Word that He will never leave nor forsake us.[2] When difficult times invade our lives, we must try our best to lean on and trust in Him. The Lord Jesus said in Luke 18:1 "that men always ought to pray and not lose heart."

If we have breath in our bodies, there are times when life will cause us grief and difficulty. But we are not without a Savior, One Who rescues.

Jesus said in John 14:33, "These things I have spoken to you, that in Me you may have peace. In the world, you will have tribulation; but be of good cheer, I have overcome the world."

May we find ourselves on our knees.

[1] **Psalm 63:3**
[2] **Hebrews 13:5**

Intent

If you a feeling a certain way, the intent of this book is too personalized; if it could be, your feelings to bring forth the mindset of hope.

There is always hope, no matter how dark and gloomy life may get.

Each day can bring forth a new beginning.

Jewels of the Heart

Grab on tight to hope, and do not let it go, so it will not be lost.

When we are girded with the Master's love, eternal death cannot have us.

Let peace take over our minds so that confusion has no place.

Joy is our strength; try not to lose it.

Always stay in the Father's face. He is the One who knows our paths.

Let your feet be guided by the Light of the World. It is in His light that we see the light.

Remember, life has its uncertainties, but Jesus

remains the same.

The breath of life is within us, so speak, to bring forth life.

Scripture said to love your neighbor; first, we must see our neighbor.

Reckless living brings forth reckless results.

Always be aware of your fruit of life because a fruit inspector sees all and knows all.

Call on the power of grace – this is life from the Father above.

What concerns are so deep that the Father of Heaven cannot solve?

Not my will, but Your will be done. Keep this in the forefront of our minds: the will of God is the betterment of us all.

He has crowned us with life; do not remove your crown by life-threatening decisions.

Let peace be the mark of your soul – it will bring forth joy.

Forgiveness is a release from the Spirit of God.

Sometimes, we can make our own beds hard by our foolish choices.

The design of our lives is not in the hands of another but only in the hands of our Maker.

When in trouble, reach out to God. He is the only One that can help you; there is deliverance in no other.

Remember the Name of Jesus; it is in His Name that we have salvation, no greater name.

The power of love will sustain us.

Jesus Christ is the author of life.

Breath of Life

What is this breath that You have breathed in us? It is Your breath that sustains us through life.

He said in His word that He has created us in His image and likeness. Wow! What manner of love is this that You have created us in this way? Your desire is that all men are to be born of Your Spirit to be able to walk in the likeness of Jesus Christ – who is the Savior of the world.

Born of His love and sustained by His grace. Having to live in His purpose to make known His love bestowed upon us. The Lord has covered us in His mercies and His lovingkindness. We are to rest in His bosom.

Thank You for Your breath that lives within us and this great love that You have given to us – this Spirit of life.

Can one measure love or maintain grace? This Spirit has no limits, helping us through our pilgrimage.

Lord, thank You for breathing in and upon us – You have blessed us with life that we may, in turn, bless You. This is love. Your breath is love, joy, and peace within our hearts.

We want to walk in Your Spirit. We want to walk in Your love. We want Your life. Great is Your love for us.

Thank You, Lord Jesus. God so loved the world, so He sent You. You have shown us the way, the truth, and the life because You love God and us. What manner of love is this? Cannot hold it – cannot stop it - cannot contain it or even wrap it up. This love is immeasurable, and it is for all. This love came from the One who first loved us.

May we bask in Your love? May we rest in Your bosom? We desire to live in Your love. It is in Jesus we have peace. May we walk with You, Lord? May we live by Your Spirit? May our hearts hope like Your heart? May we have Your joy to fill our hearts? We want to live like You, Lord Jesus. How can this be without You? Lord Jesus, You are our breath. Yes, it is the breath of life.

Great are You, Lord. Our Father who gave life. Lord, we are so grateful for this breath of life.

Thank You, Lord Jesus.

What is your understanding
of the breath of life?

_____

_____

_____

_____

_____

_____

_____

_____

_____

_____

_____

_____

_____

_____

_____

What is the evidence of the Holy Spirit in your life?

_____

_____

_____

_____

_____

_____

_____

_____

_____

_____

_____

_____

_____

_____

_____

_____

All Things are Possible

The Bible tells me all things are possible – does that include me?

How far will my mind drive me – I can jump over the hurdles of life because I know all things are possible.

What trap – no trap – what do I see – a long road in life, just waiting for me.

Are those my dreams on the left, or are those my dreams on the right? All possibilities are for me.

The Lord Jesus asked how far can you see? It will not be long, just stay with Me. Because I know He is the King, you see. Your dreams were carefully planned by Me, said He.

Hold on, do not let go; let Me guide you through those hurdles that you see.

I am Lord, I am King, I can make it all possible.

What are you believing God for that has not come to pass yet?

_____

_____

_____

_____

_____

_____

_____

_____

_____

_____

_____

_____

_____

_____

_____

_____

Trust God, and do not lose heart.

What is Faith

Does it disappear when trouble comes my way? Is it a fleeting moment when my heart is in distress? Does it fall from my hands when my hands seem to tremble?

What is this faith that God is requiring of me?

How do I know that I have it when stress is at my door?

Oh Lord, I am hurting, but do I believe I am unsure? Is it a fragile thing when my heart is beating out of control? Where is it, when my mind cannot seem to grasp and lay hold of this unruly feeling?

Father, do I believe when I do not know if I believe?

At this moment in time, all I can do is cry out to my Father, asking where are You?

Is faith something I can hold on to and press so dearly to my heart?

They tell me not to look at what I see, but does it make sense to my mind when it is hard for me to breathe.

Hold on, they say, do not let go. Oh, my Father, how am I to know?

Even in the entanglement of my misunderstanding, I could still see. Lord, You are still with me.

Loving me so kindly and tender to my heart. Who is that One holding me so I will not fall apart?

I smell the sweet fragrance of hope. I am so pleased.

I hear my Father's heartbeat so tenderly to my heart, saying daughter, I have you do not fall apart.

What is this great love that I can hardly understand?

I believe in Your love, I believe in Your word, I believe in Your tender mercies for me.

The light shines brightly, making me know and understand that You are my peace during times of chaos.

I love You because You first loved me. Oh, yes, I believe.

I can walk through the troubles with faith in my heart, knowing that You will never part.

Thank You, Father, thank You, Lord, I realize that You have restored my faith.

Who is this Jesus that loves me so? Who is the Lamb of God? I want to know.

What situation(s) in your life has caused your faith to capsize?

_____

_____

_____

_____

_____

_____

_____

_____

_____

_____

_____

_____

_____

_____

_____

_____

_____

How did God restore your faith?

Why am I Still in Chains

I remember running through my homeland, dressed in the cloth of liberty. Having the wind blow a sweet fragrance of freedom on me.

Meadows of dark green tender grass as tall as an oak tree; feeling so free in my mind, wondering what mama has fixed for dinner, wondering what chores that papa has waiting for me, thinking to himself, I am going to get that boy; he is running late. I know mama is calling for me, but it is now way past dinner time; where could he be? Having careless thoughts of me, doesn't that boy know that it is getting late? Where could he be?

I feel so trapped. What is this net over me? Where did it come from? I see someone who does not look like me. Terror and panic filled my heart. I am so confused;

what is happening to me? Who are you, what do you want? Why is this net over me? So many questions, where are they taking me?

Papa, help me; where is my momma? Don't they know that I am being snatched from them? Never to smell the sweet fragrance of my mother, never to feel those momma squeezes again. Listening and not listening to the wise instructions of my father, praying that I can hear him again.

What are these vast waters, as far as the eyes can imagine? What monstrous canoe that I am now chained to. I have chains around my ankles, so bruised, black, and blue. What is this contraption around my neck? It is hard as steel and cold as ice. I cannot move my hands! Where is my freedom? What is happening to me?

I am standing on a butcher block for all eyes to see. Why are these chains still holding me?

I am now in the 21st century, thinking that I am free, relaxed, and homebound; why are these chains still holding me? Do I fear for my life when I see a man in blue, or do I salute him and say how do you do? My neighborhood is filled with crime, and bullets are sharp as knives; why must I fear for my life when you look like I do?

Feeling so hopeless, so lost and blue. Not recognizing that unlimited power that lives within me - what must I do? I must reach down inside me and connect with that life source that lies dormant in me. This power is so vast and not able to be chained; oh, what a miracle that lies within me – the hope of glory, so faithful and true.

The Father above, who created me, has endowed me with such unbounding love that has set me free. He calls me free; He calls me love; he calls me His beloved. How can I connect to this unbounding love within me to this vast, greatness, unyielding love that has set me free? Thank You for setting me free and giving me life that can only be identified with Christ.

Thank you for loving me.

Have you ever felt as though you were bound by chains?

_____

_____

_____

_____

_____

_____

_____

_____

_____

_____

_____

_____

_____

_____

_____

_____

_____

_____

Do you know that God is a deliverer of those things that captivated you? Pray and listen to the Holy Spirit's directions.

_____

_____

_____

_____

_____

_____

_____

_____

_____

_____

_____

_____

_____

_____

_____

Why am I Feeling This Way

As I was waking up, I found myself down in the dumps. I had to ask myself why, when a treasure of life is living within me.

The man called Jesus is watching over me. He has already dispatched His angels to surround me. I must ask myself, what is the dismal feeling stirring inside me? Do I dare to make a choice to stand up in grace, that sweet incense of life that was freely given to me? I called on the Name of Jesus out of my belly of despair and began to realize the joy that was graciously given to me. I have hope; I must reach out and grab it. Why? Because this choice is up to me. I grabbed hold of the living Word of life to change my heart's desire. I now sense His presence, which is always with me. I command my soul to speak life to my life. I continuously cry out to Jesus Christ, who is the Son of the living God.

The Prince of Peace inspired my soul. He is the Mighty God that rescued me.

Isaiah 9:6; "For unto us a Child is born, unto us a Son is given; and the government will be upon His shoulder. And His name will be called Wonderful, Counselor, Mighty God, Everlasting Father, Prince of Peace."

Try Him!

Depression is real.
Do you have any suicidal thoughts?
Did you reach out for help?

How is your mental status now?

_____

_____

_____

_____

_____

_____

_____

_____

_____

_____

_____

_____

_____

_____

If your mental status has not changed – Get help from a Certified Mental Health Provider.

Deep Sea Diving

Put on your gear and dive into the waters of life.

Pouncing into these sweet waters, feeling so free in the freshness of your soul.

As you go diving into this way – envision these waters covering you from head to toe.

As you submerge in this ocean of love, sense the hugs from the heart of Jesus to your heart. He is the Shepherd and Bishop of your soul.[1] Deeper and deeper into the Word you go, offering you the unmeasurable thirst for the life of God. Wondering if I would ever be satisfied? "Yes, said He, because you are anchored in My soul. "

These waters of life – into the Word you go. The presence of God surrounds you with the warm embrace of His love. Deep sea diving into the Word will bring forth blessings of the Father, more than one could ever realize. Do I ever have to leave these calm, soothing waters that are refreshing to me? Then I heard a tender, loving voice, 'no, My child, because I love you so. I gave My life for you, didn't you know? I covered you in My love and gave you peace. Stay in these waters, this ocean of life, smothered by goodness, joy, and no strife.'

'With these waters of love, wherein I offer you – herein in is my grace, yes, My life.'

Jesus is He who sits High on the throne, covering me with His strong arms so gracefully warm.

Gliding through these bountiful waters, these still calm waters, all for the living – offering life. In these waters, you will find My grace and love for You.

Join me in these waters – the waters of life.

¹ Peter 2:25

Are you acquainted with the Word of God?

_____

_____

_____

_____

_____

_____

_____

_____

_____

_____

_____

_____

_____

_____

_____

_____

If acquainted with the Word of God – Do you spend time with God in His Word?

_____

_____

_____

_____

_____

_____

_____

_____

_____

_____

_____

_____

_____

_____

_____

_____

_____

_____

Go deep sea diving with the Holy Spirit – see how He will change your life.

_____

_____

_____

_____

_____

_____

_____

_____

_____

_____

_____

_____

_____

_____

_____

_____

The Big Spirit in the Sky

The great waters must be angry. I am terrified. Am I alone in this dungeon? So dark I cannot see but hear moaning and crying from the hearts of others.

Why am I here? Something hit and hurt my head, and this put me in a deep sleep. My head is pounding with such pain I can hardly see. Every time I try to move, I hear the humongous chains trying to move with me.

What happened to my family? I do not know. Our home has been destroyed and burnt with fire.

Men with no color look so angry – why are they angry? Did I do something to them? I just went out to get food for my family. When I came back, my family was gone, and my poppa was found dead. What happened? Why, Big Spirit in the Sky?

Oh, there is a little dim light in the big hole that is never-ending. I see so many pearly Black men that look like me as far as I can see. We speak different tongues of the mouth but speak the same tongue in our eyes and hearts.

I hear fear when I look at them. Skin is pearly black like mine. Oh, what stench. Big Spirit in the Sky, please help me.

For some reason, I am not afraid, should be but not. The Big Spirit in the Sky is with me, carrying me through these desperate waters. Waters, are you angry with me? I began to speak with them that look like me, 'don't be afraid, the Big Spirit in the Sky is with us.'

They do not seem to understand, but I will continue to tell them.

Big Spirit in the Sky, I never thought to ask Your name. What is Your name? I want to know; I need to know.

"My Name is Jesus; I will never leave nor forsake you."[1]

---

[1] **Hebrews 13:5**

Do you know the name(s) of God?

_____

_____

_____

_____

_____

_____

_____

_____

_____

_____

_____

_____

_____

_____

_____

_____

_____

What is your personal name for God?

Do you have an intimate relationship with Jesus Christ?

My Cry to the One who Hears

Can I cry out to a God that I do not know but I need to know.

My life is filled with many disappointments and seems void of the spring of life. Where is the hope – I need to have hope.

How can I reach out to God when it seems as though my heart is filled with this harsh sound of emptiness?

I cannot cry out – but I need to cry out.

Lord, will You hear me when I am not sure about You? How far will my cry go? Will it reach the heavens? God, may my unsounding cry reach Your heart, and would You incline Your ear to my shattered heart. Are You able to piece back together my heart?

They say that You love me – do You love me? Do You hear the voice of my heart? Will You listen to my cry?

They say that Jesus died for us all—am I included in that number?

As I lay trying to slumber and sleep, a swelling presence of innocence seemed to be wrapping around me like a blanket, securing me with a sweet aroma of life.

Do I embrace this great fulfillment of joy? Do I breathe in this unspeakable peace that has engulfed my heart?

I heard about Grace; I sense this Spirit of Grace. I abound in this Spirit of Grace.

Spirit of Grace, I gladly embrace You because You first embraced me and put a song of deliverance in my heart.

What joy and peace. God, I love You and thank You for loving me.

This Jesus I know, this Jesus whom I embrace.

I see the cross in my mind set. I joy in the cross in my heart.

I believe in You, Lord my Savior. Thank You, my Father, for this great love wherewith You have loved me.

You have embraced and touched my heart; now, my life belongs to You.

Oh, what joy! You have covenanted with me to bring me into eternal life.

Thank You for loving me and for taking care of me.

This strong love I even dare to embrace and not to let go.

Strange how You love me and why, I will never know.

Thank You, my Lord for this I could not pay.

Grace has abounded in me, and to never let go.

Great is Your faithfulness, and I surely enjoy Your

sweet presence that has given me life.

Thank You Father

Thank You, Lord Jesus

Thank You, Holy Spirit.

Have you ever cried out to God and did not think He heard you?

_____

_____

_____

_____

_____

_____

_____

_____

_____

_____

_____

_____

_____

_____

_____

_____

_____

The Scriptures said that "He never slumber or sleep." Psalm 121.

How did God answer you to let you know that He heard you?

_____

_____

_____

_____

_____

_____

_____

_____

_____

_____

_____

_____

_____

_____

_____

_____

_____

_____

He Who Wore a Crown of Thorns

My eyes were closed tightly shut, and seeing Him on the cross, wondering to myself was all lost. The most beautiful crown of thorns was visible on His head, even though it was bloody red.

How can I deny a love that is so strong?

Saw those thorns, pressed so deep in His skull, was that possible when there were no tears shed at all. In heartfelt agony, the thorns were raging in His head. He in His royalty, looked at me all the long.

Great is Your faithfulness, great is Your love, with that crown of thorns that outweighed the brightness of the stars above. Would it be okay if I reached up and touched the crown of thorns so strategically arranged on Your head, sensing Your love that is ever so strong?

How can this be? The man Christ Jesus has such love for me.

Glancing and seeing those thorns made me realize the loveliness that all men may have to live on. Grace and elegance circling his head – what magnificence all robed in red. I saw the awesomeness of crimson, the glory of scarlet, the glamor of rubies all dancing about His head.

What was that thorn of crowns? It was hard for me to imagine what took root in my head. Oh, such exquisiteness, so dazzling, that crown of thorns arrayed in the waterfall of red.

I opened my eyes very quickly to see the glorious wonder of all is to be. Now I see many crowns so brilliant, so gorgeous– too glittering for my eyes to behold. There was the glamour of rubies, the grandeur of emeralds, the elegance of topaz, and much richness of all the gems that can be.

He is the King of glory, the Lord of lords. He reigns in majesty on His throne for all the world to see. Great is the glory of our God, sitting on a throne with the essence of the crown of love.

When you close your eyes, can you picture Jesus? Describe what you see in your mind's eye.

_____

_____

_____

_____

_____

_____

_____

_____

_____

_____

_____

_____

_____

_____

_____

_____

Up from the Ashes

I keep looking back because of the frightfulness of my past that keeps chasing me. I want to be free of these lost memories.

Thinking in my head, why did I do this? Why did I walk that unseemly path? Why didn't I change my environment, place, and things? Why did I reach out for those things that have caused me harm? Why is my past following me?

My past and my failures are taking over my thoughts, trying to change my future. What obstacle is in front of me and even surrounding me? What must I do about these raging fires that are clogging my mind?

So, I cry out to the One who knows my past and He who holds my future.

I asked the question, "why are You evading me?" "Are you present with me?"

My thoughts haunt me; my life is in a deadly entrapment.

So, again, I cry out, "Where are You?"

These things that are around me seem to be in a dark place. "Where are You?" Then I begin to know and understand that You were in my past, You are in my present, and You will meet me in my future."

So, my hope began to rise out of the dust of ashes to know that You are the God of my life. Then, I began to obtain the everlasting knowledge that I was never alone.

You have walked me through the dismal places of life and brought me sunshine, but I just could not see.

Now, I understand that You are my peace – the Rock of my salvation. My hope is in You, and You gave me the courage to believe. You spoke love to my heart. You are the One who calmed my mind. At first, I could not see, but now I do.

You are the hope of glory; You stopped the waters of despair from smothering me and reached out to breathe breath into my body. You said to me, "I love you."

Who is this One that is Jesus – who is this One that saved me?

You brought life to me when I did not understand life and gave me hope. I am born from above because You spoke it so.

You said to me that, "You are from everlasting to everlasting." You are the One that shaped the world into being and developed the heavens. You placed the stars in magnificent order and spoke to the sun and moon, and they came to be.

Who is this One that is Almighty and holds me in His heart? Who brought grace into my life so that I may walk in the path of hope?

Discourage, I am not because You are with me and never to leave me alone.

I know that I am dearly loved by the One who first loved me.

Thank You, my Savior – thank You, my joy – thank You, my Lord Jesus Christ.

How has the Holy Spirit changed your life?

_____

_____

_____

_____

_____

_____

_____

_____

_____

_____

_____

_____

_____

_____

_____

_____

_____

Have others noticed the change in you?

_____

_____

_____

_____

_____

_____

_____

_____

_____

_____

_____

_____

_____

_____

_____

_____

_____

The Sea of Life

These hurricanic waters are all around me. I am descending in these vast waters of life. Lord, I am being tossed up and down; even those frosting white foams from the deep blue waters are covering my head.

In order for me not to go down into the depths of the sea and lose hope in these waters of despair, I must tap into the life source that the Father has so delicately placed in me called perseverance. Not having the choice but to give up on this desire to live.

Remembering that I am made in the image and likeness of He who has brought me forth from the bowels of His love. I must recall to my mind that the Great One loves me with everlasting love. While in the sea of despair, I must also put to my remembrance this magnificent, glorious grace that gives me life.

I must hold on to this anchor called hope and never let it go!

Lord, do You see these waves billowing over my head? The white foams from this vast sea cloud my view of Your love for me. I must call on Your name, Lord Jesus, for You are my salvation. Your Word, Lord, is the anchor for my soul. My Lord Jesus, I remember of old how I was told that You are my help. They said to me just call on His name.

So, while I am being grafted in these waters of despair,

I cry out, "Jesus, Jesus, my Lord and Savior. I need Your help."

Then, out of the depths of my soul, I hear, "I am with you, My child; I have never left nor forsaken you. I am greater than those waters of despair; I am your hope when things seem hopeless. Remember Me, remember My love for you because you are my chosen child."

Through my eyes of intimacy from years long ago, I see those desperate waters of despair dissipating from the depths of my mind. Now, my Lord, I can breathe the fresh air of restoration. I feel Your presence all around me, enlightening my heart. Thank You for loving me, for You are my deliver, and You are my hope. Life is worth living because it is the absolute gift from the Savior of mankind.

Lord Jesus, You are my anchor of life.

My soul cries out in the foam of harmony and peace. Lord, You are the treasure of my heart. My God is the rock of my salvation. I hear the waves of peace revitalizing my heart and soul. Now, I know that I may live and not die. ***Hello life***.

Thank You, Lord Jesus Christ -- my Savior, my life.

Have you ever felt like you were in desperate need of help?

_____

_____

_____

_____

_____

_____

_____

_____

_____

_____

_____

_____

_____

_____

_____

_____

_____

How did you get the help
that you needed?

Mister Man

Hey, mister man, you say that you love me – can I stand up in this love and be ever so free?

Mister man, do you see the purpose that God has placed in me? Lover, can I trust you with my heart – you promised that we will never part.

Mister man, as I walk by your side, will I feel confident, because you called me your bride?

I see those muscular arms and I cannot wait, cannot wait until they get around me. Holding me so close makes me feel so secure.

Mister man, do I have your trust? I see how you walk in a room – my eyes cannot turn away thinking that you belong to me.

I do not know; not sure do you love me.

You hold my heart, make me smile, Mister man, can I trust you?

Mister man, I see how you wear that hat tipped to the side - nobody can walk with that bold stride.

Mister man, will you build me up or tear me down? Mister man, you are my crown.

Mister man, do you honor me? Can I trust you; whether I bore your children or not, do you have my best interest? Do you have my back?

Who can I lean on when I need to talk? Is that you Mister Man? Will you listen to me with your heart?

Will you encourage and build me up so I feel like I can walk on the moon, or will you bring me down so that I feel I cannot get up again? Mister man, how will you treat me? I must know whether I can feel secure with you.

Mister Man, Mister Man, I do love you.

Trust in the Lord with all your heart and lean not on your own understanding. In all your ways, acknowledge Him, and He shall direct your paths. [1]

[1] [1]**Proverbs 3:5-6**

Are you in a healthy relationship?

The Scriptures said that Jesus is closer than a brother: Proverbs 18:24. How do you know that Jesus is close to you?

_____

_____

_____

_____

_____

_____

_____

_____

_____

_____

_____

_____

_____

_____

_____

Do You Know

Just in case you do not know Him, let me tell you about Him.

God is love. Did you know that God our Father gave His only begotten Son for the remission of our sins? Did you know in 1 Timothy 1:17, written in the halls of eternity, that God is the "King eternal, immortal, invisible, He is the only wise God, be honor and glory forever and ever." Did you know that in Revelation 4:11, it was stated, "You are worthy, O Lord, to receive glory and honor and power; for You have created all things, and by Your will they exist and were created." Can you imagine the One with all glory and honor offers humankind life and hope – because of His love for us. This God walks with us through our trials and tribulations. See Isaiah 43:2; "When you pass through the waters, I will be with you; and through the rivers, they shall not overflow you. When you walk through the fire, you shall not be burned, nor shall the flame scorch you." Remember that in all your beloved years, He has never failed you. To this King of Glory, hold on for life eternal - it behooves us not to let go! The One, the Eternal King, desires a close relationship with His children.

Jesus said I am the way, the truth, and the life. No one comes to the Father except through Me.[1]

[1] John 14:6

What do you know about God?

_____

_____

_____

_____

_____

_____

_____

_____

_____

_____

_____

_____

_____

_____

_____

_____

_____

Do you realize the love that Jesus has for you? How did you come to that conclusion?

_____

_____

_____

_____

_____

_____

_____

_____

_____

_____

_____

_____

_____

_____

_____

_____

_____

_____

Love is not the color of my Skin

My skin is pearly white; my skin is jet black as coal.

Does God love me? Yes, He does, does God live in me. Yes, He does.

So why cannot we love each other.

Love is not the color of my skin – but the life in my heart.

My soul, will you reject hatred and embrace love? Will we walk in peace as God graciously commanded us to do so?

Will I make the determination to love my brethren?

Why hurt me --- I will not hurt you. Father, will you remove the blinders from my eyes so that I may see the blood of Jesus -- this blood that was shed for all men.

May we see through the cross, not the burning cross of men, but through and by the cross of Jesus Christ, the Lord who now is seated on His throne.

Have you ever been discriminated against?

Have you ever made an error of choice against someone because of the color of their skin or someone being different?

_____

_____

_____

_____

_____

_____

_____

_____

_____

_____

_____

_____

_____

_____

_____

_____

_____

Saved by Him

I was drowning in a sea of despair. Was there anyone to help me? Why didn't anyone see my pain? I had on my life jacket of self-righteousness, but it was to no avail. The waves of self-loathe covered me. I tried to hold on, but again, to no avail.

In a matter of moments when I thought all was loss! A sweet incense of life covered me. It was the smell of honey on the rock. Now, the sea of despair had become the sea of hope. This life jacket had become the righteousness of Christ. It is in Him; I live and move and have my being.[1] The hope of glory had come to save me. Who is this Savior they call Christ? It is Jesus, the Son of the living God. I was told in Acts 4:12; "Nor is there salvation in any other, for there is no other name under heaven given among men by which we must be saved." The name of Jesus is where our life resides.

I am now a witness to the love of Jesus Christ. He said in John 14:6; "I am the way, the truth, and the life..." Lord by Your Holy Spirit, take me the way, teach me Your truth that I may have Your life. My life jacket has changed to the righteousness of Christ. I am now living in hope.

You are my Lord, You are my Savior, and I thank You for saving me, and I know without any doubt You are

Jesus Christ.

Thank You, Lord, for loving me.

[1] **Acts 17:28**

Have you ever had an encounter with Jesus? Explain.

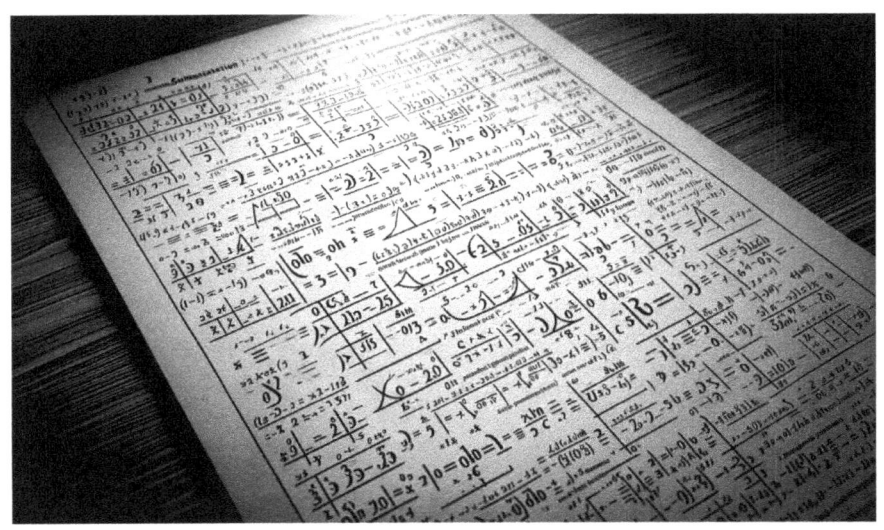

Sum of it All

In the book of Ecclesiastes, Solomon wrote, "Let us hear the conclusion of the whole matter: Fear God and keep His commandments: for this is the whole duty of man. For God shall bring every work into judgment, with every secret thing, whether it be good, or whether it be evil."[1]

Yes, what is the conclusion of the matter – have we arrived with our fancy cars and big houses and have no love? Where does that leave us?

Can we claim my job is on the one – Thank you, Jesus, for my job, car, home, and family and have no love, where does that leave us?

Do these physical matters fulfill my heart? Do these

things take the place of the fulfillment of love

Lord, may I ask You where are my treasures? Is my life filled with the bountifulness of the things, or is it You? Where do You reside in my heart?

Does my peace come from You or the things that You have blessed me with?

How do I give You glory, Lord?

How is the longing in my heart complete? Is it in what You have given me, or is it You?

Can or will the Spirit of grace help me to find the answer.

What is the driving force of my longing for You, Lord? Is it spiritual, or is it physical?

Can these things of the earth satisfy me without You being a part of these things of the earth?

My God, I am crying out to You, where is my longing - what will satisfy my soul.

Is it You? I am not sure?

[1] **Ecclesiastes 12:13-14**

Has the earthly treasure ever captured your heart?

What Scripture helped you to get free from those things that held you in bondage?

_____

_____

_____

_____

_____

_____

_____

_____

_____

_____

_____

_____

_____

_____

_____

The Treasure of Life

This span of life is evermore, so be careful how you treat it.

This life that I have given you is a blessing from Me.

I am the Highest of the Highest.

The breath that you breathe is from Me.

I have chosen life for you; know that this blessing comes from Me.

IF you allow Me, let Me guide you through this path of life.

Do not throw away what I have given to you.

Treat your life with kindness, and always ponder the grace of love.

Love is the master key of this life treasure that I have given you.

Walk in peace, dance in joy, and try to laugh ever more.

Life is a blessing – a blessing from Me.

Manage it with care—treat yourself with patience – this life I have given you is from Me.

Love yourself because I love you.

Let this love overflow – that you may touch even those

you may not know.

Life is precious – again, manage it with care.

You are blessed – this is something I have given to you.

Honor life – that you may honor another.

Love life- that you may love another.

Life is a gift – treat it as though.

Life, I have given to you – it is something you cannot manage on your own. Give it back to Me.

Treasure and love what I have given to you. Will you walk in this blessing – for I am with you.

Write your own words of wisdom.

_____

_____

_____

_____

_____

_____

_____

_____

_____

_____

_____

_____

_____

_____

_____

_____

_____

_____

What is your favorite Scripture?

Love is our Manifesto

What is a manifesto?

Webster defined it as a public declaration of intentions, motives, or views.

Can you imagine this imaginary conversation?

God said "I want my people to know that love is majestic." One of the angels responded to the Father, "how can You say that love is majestic?" God – "It is written in the library of life in James 2:8, that I said, "that My people are to fulfill the royal law which is love." The seraphim responded, "how interesting." God preceded to tell the host of heaven, remember what My Son said about love. All the angels and the host of heaven shouted with excitement and joy and said, "What did our Lord, Jesus the Christ, say?" God the Father answered, "well remember in John 15:13, My Son said, "Greater love has no one than this than to lay down one's life for His friends." Suddenly, there appeared a regal purple illumination that glowed throughout the heavens. Then came Jesus from around the corner of the galaxies and said, "What is all this commotion throughout the skies." God said, "it is because of You, My Son." "Thank You for dying on the cross for My people." Remember, there is no greater love from the Father through Jesus by the Holy Spirit. God loves us!

No matter what life hands us, remember the royal love of the Father.

How do you respond to the command of love when it is not easy to submit to submit one to another?

_____

_____

_____

_____

_____

_____

_____

_____

_____

_____

_____

_____

_____

_____

_____

_____

_____

_____

He who Lives

I am He who lives evermore; I am from the days of old – behold, I am from everlasting to everlasting; I hold all times of now and will meet you in your future.

I have robed and wrapped Myself in splendor, waiting for all the world to see.

I have created the day and brought light into the darkness; I open the dawn of the morning and close the curtain of the night.

Nothing surpasses My understanding – I am the One who gives life, and the author of it. My peace is the true essence of every being.

Grace is My crown of glory – love is My robe of righteousness.

I set the sun and moon in its place for I am the designer of the host of heaven.

I left My Spirit to guide you through this pathway of life.

I was in the yesterday; I am in the now and will be in what will come.

My joy is everlasting – will you come to Me?

I am Jesus the Christ.

What encouraging words have the Holy Spirit spoken to you?

_____

_____

_____

_____

_____

_____

_____

_____

_____

_____

_____

_____

_____

_____

_____

_____

God loves you.

Suicidal Hot Line

If you feel as though you need medical attention because you cannot shake depression or suicidal thoughts. Reach out to a Mental Health Care Provider.

The Word of God said in I Peter 2:24: "Who Himself bore our sins in His own body on the tree, that we, having died to sins, might live for righteousness – by whose stripes you were healed."

God, through Jesus Christ, heals through various avenues.

Sometimes, the only prayer we can say is "God help."

Suicidal Hotline 24 hours: 988

Prayers

Blessings

Heavenly Father,

I am asking You to touch every person who has read this book of poems so that their lives may be enriched through Your loving presence.

Thank You, Lord Jesus, for giving Your life on the cross and according to Hebrews 7:25; You are making intercession for us. How wonderful it is that You are still praying for us.

Thank You for Your love and grace.

In Jesus' Name.

Hopefully, you have accepted Jesus Christ as your Lord and Savior, if not, will you at this very moment pray and ask the Lord Jesus to enter your heart that He may be your Lord and Savior.

To the person(s) reading this book, I speak blessings of peace in your heart, mind, and soul.

Protection

Father God, thank You that Your word tells us that he who dwells in the secret place of the Most-High shall abide under the shadow of the Almighty. It is an honor to be able to dwell with You in that secret place and to have You as our refuge and fortress, our God in You we trust.

Surely You shall deliver us from the snare of the fowler and from the perilous pestilence, and we are grateful for deliverance. Father, You said in Your word that we shall be covered with Your feathers and under Your wings is our refuge. Your truth is our shield and buckler. Because of Your protection over us, we shall not be afraid of the terror by night, nor of the arrow that flies by day, nor of the pestilence that walks in the darkness, nor of the destruction that lays waste at noonday. For this, we give You all the glory and honor.

Yes, a thousand may fall at our side and ten thousand at our right hand; but it shall not come near us. Only with our eyes shall we look and see the reward of the wicked. Thank You for Your protection over us.

Lord, You are our refuge, the Most High, our dwelling place; there shall no evil befall us, nor shall any plague come near our dwelling. Because You shall give Your angels charge over us and, in their hands, they shall bear us up, unless we dash our foot against a stone. Because of Your goodness, we shall tread on the lion and cobra, the young lion, and the serpent we shall trample underfoot. Thank You, oh Most High.[1]

In Jesus' Name.

Psalm 91

The Lord's written response and promise to the Psalmist in Psalm 91:

"Because he has set his love upon Me, therefore I will deliver him; I will set him on high because he has known My name. He shall call upon Me, and I will answer him; I will be with him in trouble; I will deliver him and honor him. With long life, I will satisfy him and show him My salvation."

To God be the Glory

Peace

Definition of Peace:

Zondervan Illustrated Bible Dictionary: The word used in the OT (Heb. *salom*) basically means "completeness" or "soundness." According to the NT, peace (Gr. *eirene*) results from God's forgiveness and is the ideal relation among believers.

In the New Compact Bible Dictionary peace is also used throughout the Bible to indicate a spirit of tranquility and freedom from either inward or outward disturbance.

The Merriam-Webster Dictionary: Freedom from disturbing thoughts or emotions.

Father, we come before You, acknowledging You are God and asking You to fill our hearts with peace. Your word said, "You will keep us in perfect peace whose minds are steadfast because we trust in You." [1]May we learn to grab hold of the peace that You have given to us during our times of unrest. Thank You, Lord, for blessing us with this sustainable peace. Lord, You said, "peace I leave with you, my peace I give to you; not as the world gives do I give to you and let not your heart be troubled, neither let it be afraid."[2] You have given us quiet and tranquility during our difficult and frightful times. We are not going to give our hearts or minds permission to be stressful or unrestful. We are to "let Your peace rule in our hearts, to be thankful." [3] and to "allow peace to take root in our hearts. Holy Spirit help us to be gentle to all men that others may know that our Father is at hand. We are not to be anxious for anything but in everything by prayer and supplication to be thankful."[4] Great is Your faithfulness. "When our ways please You Lord, You will make our enemies to be at peace with us." [5]The greatest joy is that we may be at peace with You and allow peace to cover and protect us like a warm, snuggly blanket. This peace comes from Your great love for us; there is no greater love. God, we need Your peace to take rule in our hearts and to guide us through this journey of life that can sometimes be unruly.

Thank You, Father, for giving us peace.

In Jesus' Name.

[1] Isaiah 26:3
[2] John 14:27
[3] Colossians 3:15
[4] Philippians 4:5-6
[5] Proverbs 16:7

Guidance

Guidance from the Good Shepherd. Who is the Good Shepherd? Jesus Christ is the Shepherd.

John 10:11: "I am the good shepherd; the good shepherd gives His life for the sheep."

I Peter 2:25: For you were like sheep going astray but have now returned to the Shepherd and Overseer of your souls.

Lord, You are our shepherd, and we shall not want You to make us lie down in green pastures; You lead us beside the still waters. You restore our souls and lead us in the paths of righteousness, all for Your Name's sake. Yeah, though we walk through the valley or the shadow of death, we will fear no evil, for You are with us; Your rod and staff comfort us. You have prepared a table before us in the presence of our enemies; You anoint our heads with oil; our cup runs over. Surely goodness and mercy shall follow us all the days of our lives. And we dwell in the house of the Lord forever.[1]

In Jesus' Name.

[1] **Psalm 23**

Abide

Lord Jesus, You are the true vine, and God Your Father is the husbandman. Every branch in You that bears no fruit will be taken away, and every branch that does bear fruit will be pruned for the purpose of bringing forth more fruit. We are already clean because of the word that You have spoken to us. The command is to abide in You, and You will abide in us because we cannot bear fruit of ourselves unless we abide in You as the vine. You have told us that You are the vine, and we are the branches, and when we abide in You, we will bear much fruit because, without You, we can do nothing.

Father God, when we bear much fruit, You are glorified and may we pray to continue in Your love.

May we always remember and live as though we belong to You. Thank You, Father God[1].

In Jesus' Name.

[1] John 15:1-5;8-9

The Word of God

Father, may we bear the Word of God in our hearts so we may breathe love to the brethren. Your word is living and powerful and sharper than any two-edged sword, piercing even to the division of soul and Spirit, and joints and marrow, and is a discerner of the thoughts and intents of the heart[1]. Father, You are the God of our Lord Jesus Christ, the Father of glory; we pray for the Spirit of wisdom and revelation in the Knowledge of Jesus, that the eyes of our understanding being enlightened, that we may know what is the hope of Your calling, what are the riches of the glory of Your inheritance in the saints, and what is the exceeding greatness of Your power toward us who believe, according to the working of Your mighty power which You worked in Christ when You raised Him from the dead and seated Him at Your right hand in the heavenly places, far above all principality and power and might and dominion, and every name that is named, not only in this age but also in that which is to come.

And You have put all things under the feet of Jesus and gave Him to be head over all things to the church, which is the body of Jesus Christ, the fullness of Him who fills all in all.[2]

Thanks be to God in the highest.

In Jesus' Name

[1] **Hebrews 4:12**
[2] **Ephesians 1:17-23**

Remember

Remember the love of God and to love Him with all your heart, soul and mind, and we are to love our neighbor as ourselves.

Remember to love yourself that you may love others.[1]

[1] **Matthew 22: 37-39**

www.ingramcontent.com/pod-product-compliance
Lightning Source LLC
Chambersburg PA
CBHW051226120626
46547CB00013B/1529